YOSI

NATIONAL PARK

YOSEMITE

WORDSEARCH

Find and circle the words. Remember to look up, down, to the side and diagonally.

B	T	F	A	M	I	L	Y	A	S	A	M	G
I	Y	E	E	R	Y	O	S	E	M	I	T	E
R	H	L	I	K	J	L	A	B	S	Y	R	C
D	S	C	W	G	N	S	D	T	W	E	N	A
E	C	A	L	S	L	E	A	T	A	R	I	L
R	E	P	D	E	L	O	U	H	T	U	C	I
P	P	I	N	E	T	R	E	E	E	B	O	F
S	O	T	K	E	E	O	T	J	R	R	U	O
D	H	A	L	F	D	O	M	E	F	I	S	R
E	U	N	T	S	Y	E	E	E	A	V	I	N
E	X	N	C	O	E	E	R	K	L	E	N	I
R	R	A	C	T	U	N	N	E	L	R	T	A

- yosemite
- half dome
- el capitan
- deer
- coyote
- river
- bird
- tunnel
- waterfall
- pine tree
- california
- family

I spy with my little eye..

Color the things you hope to see on your trip to Yosemite

Animals I saw in Yosemite!

Yosemite is full of animals. Keep an eye out and put a checkmark next to the animals you see during your visit. There are more than are on this list so add to it if you can.

Coyote
Black Bear
Mountain Lion
Birds
Skunk
Deer
Rainbow Trout
Grey Squirrel
Ground Squirrel
Raccoon
Red-tailed hawk
Blue jay

Word scramble!

Unscramble the words.
Hint: they are all animals found in Yosemite.

yootce

rebalbkacr

rede

tturowbaniorg

kunks

mloinnaionu

orcacon

Campfire Story!

Write your own spooky campfire story and then tell your family!

Tic-Tac-Toe

Draw a Fox

Draw the fox by drawing what you see in each box.

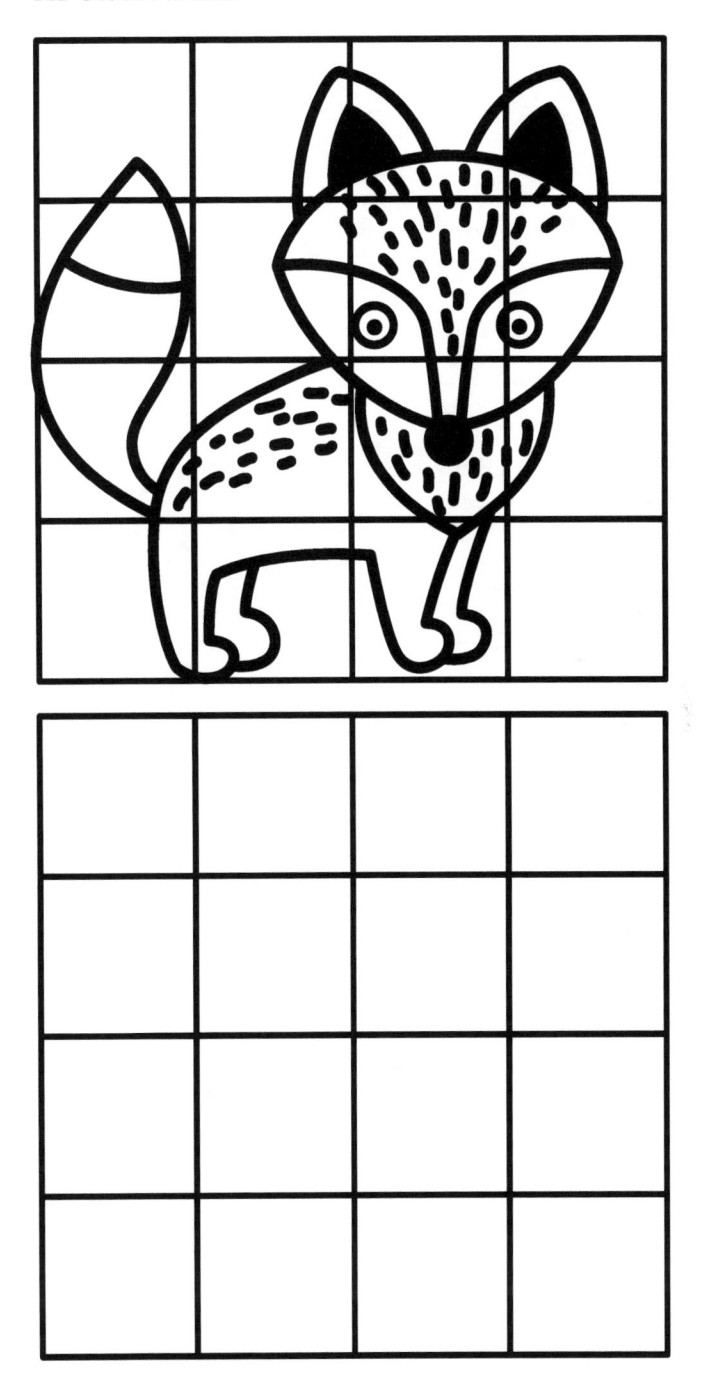

Baby Deer Maze Challenge

Help the baby deer reach her mother

Storytelling

Write a funny story about a raccoon and a skunk who went to Yosemite on vacation....

Color it!

Draw a Squirrel

Draw the squirrel by drawing what you see in each box.

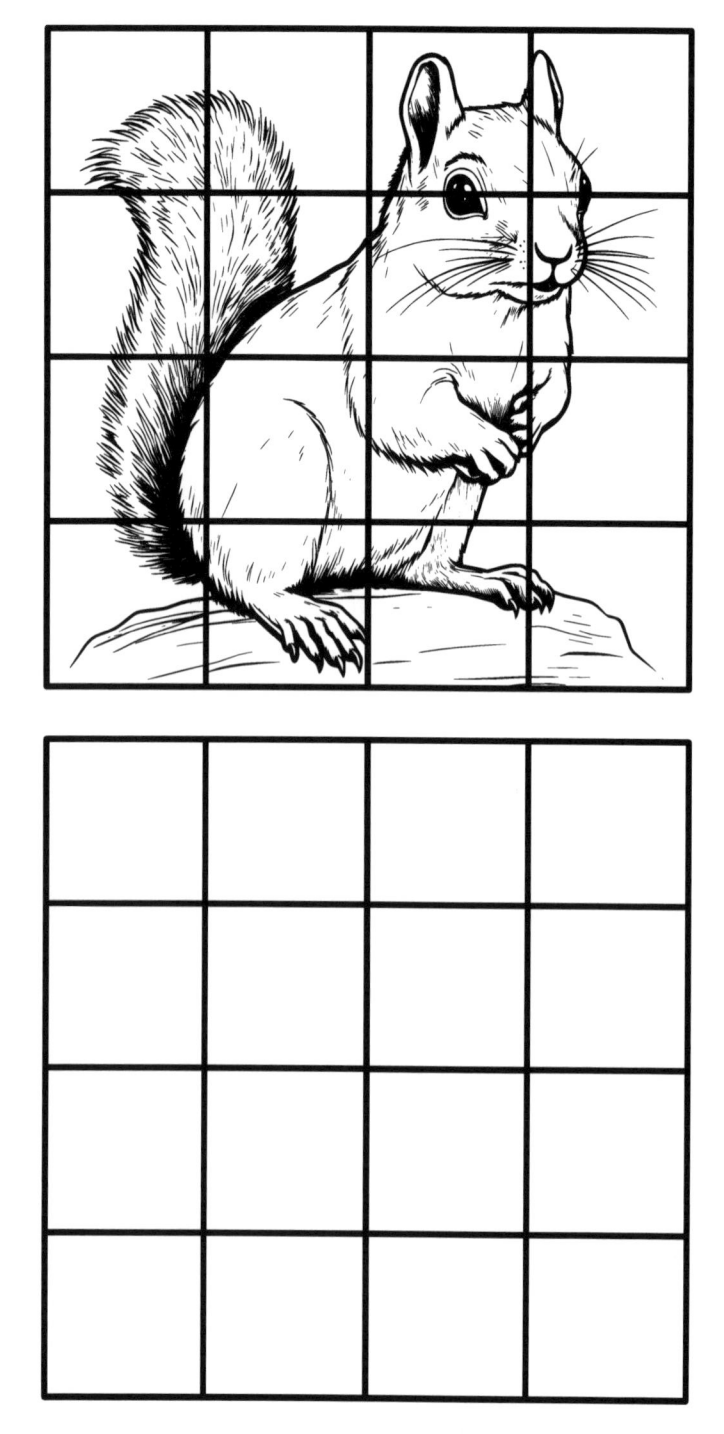

Funny animal jokes:

Why did the raccoon sleep under the car?
Because he wanted to wake up oily

What do you call a bear with no teeth?
A gummy bear!

Why did the deer get braces?
Because he had buck teeth!

Have you heard the joke about the skunk?
Never mind...it really stinks!

How can you catch a squirrel?
Climb up a tree and act like a nut!

Why did the coyote cross the road?
To eat the chicken who had crossed earlier!

What bird needs to wear a wig?
A bald eagle!

Vacation

WORDSEARCH

Find and circle the words. Remember to look up, down, to the side and diagonally.

B	T	F	A	M	I	L	Y	A	S	N	M	D
I	Y	E	E	P	Y	O	S	E	I	I	R	E
R	H	L	M	K	J	L	V	A	L	L	E	Y
B	S	A	W	G	N	S	T	T	B	E	N	A
E	C	A	N	W	O	N	A	T	A	R	I	L
A	E	I	D	E	I	O	U	H	T	U	C	I
U	P	R	N	O	T	L	E	E	E	B	A	F
T	O	P	M	E	E	O	D	J	T	R	M	O
I	H	I	L	F	V	A	C	A	T	I	O	N
F	U	A	T	S	Y	E	A	E	E	V	I	N
U	X	N	C	O	E	E	R	K	E	E	N	I
L	R	E	C	T	U	N	N	E	S	R	T	A

- vacation
- airplane
- car
- mountain
- camp
- bird
- trees
- wild
- beautiful
- canyon
- valley
- family

True or False?

Write down True or False. The answers are on the next page.

1. You should give the wild animals snacks:

2. Yosemite is in the state of Nevada

3. Raccoons are friendly animals

4. If you see a baby deer all by itself, you should take it home with you

5. Rock climbers love Yosemite

6. You should always pick up your trash

7. It's ok to drink water from the river in Yosemite

8. It's ok to swim in the river when it is rushing quickly

9. You should always stay on the trail when hiking

10. You can leave trash and food in your car when you visit Yosemite

1. FALSE. Wild animals can be dangerous and people's food is not good for them. Don't feed wild animals and don't get too close to them.

2. FALSE. Yosemite is in the state of California

3. FALSE. Raccoons are cute but they can actually be very mean. Keep your distance.

4. FALSE. Momma deer sometimes leave their babies in a hiding spot but will always come back for them.

5. TRUE. Yosemite is famous around the world for some of the best rock climbing.

6. TRUE. Wild places are beautiful and it is important not to leave our trash when we visit natural places. Pick up after yourself and if you see trash on the ground, pick it up and find a trash can... even if it isn't your trash!

7. FALSE. It is not safe to drink water from streams or rivers. There are a lot of germs and bacteria in the water so don't drink it. It could make you very sick.

8. FALSE. During spring, fall, and winter, the rivers are very dangerous. Even in the summer, some parts of the river are unsafe for swimmers. Never get too close to the water's edge.

9. TRUE. Stay on the trail so you don't get lost or separated from your group.

10. FALSE. Bears love to break into cars to steal food so don't leave any food or garbage in your car. They can rip off the doors and do a lot of damage!

Help the ranger find his way home

Color it!

Draw a Raccoon

Draw the raccoon by drawing what you see in each box.

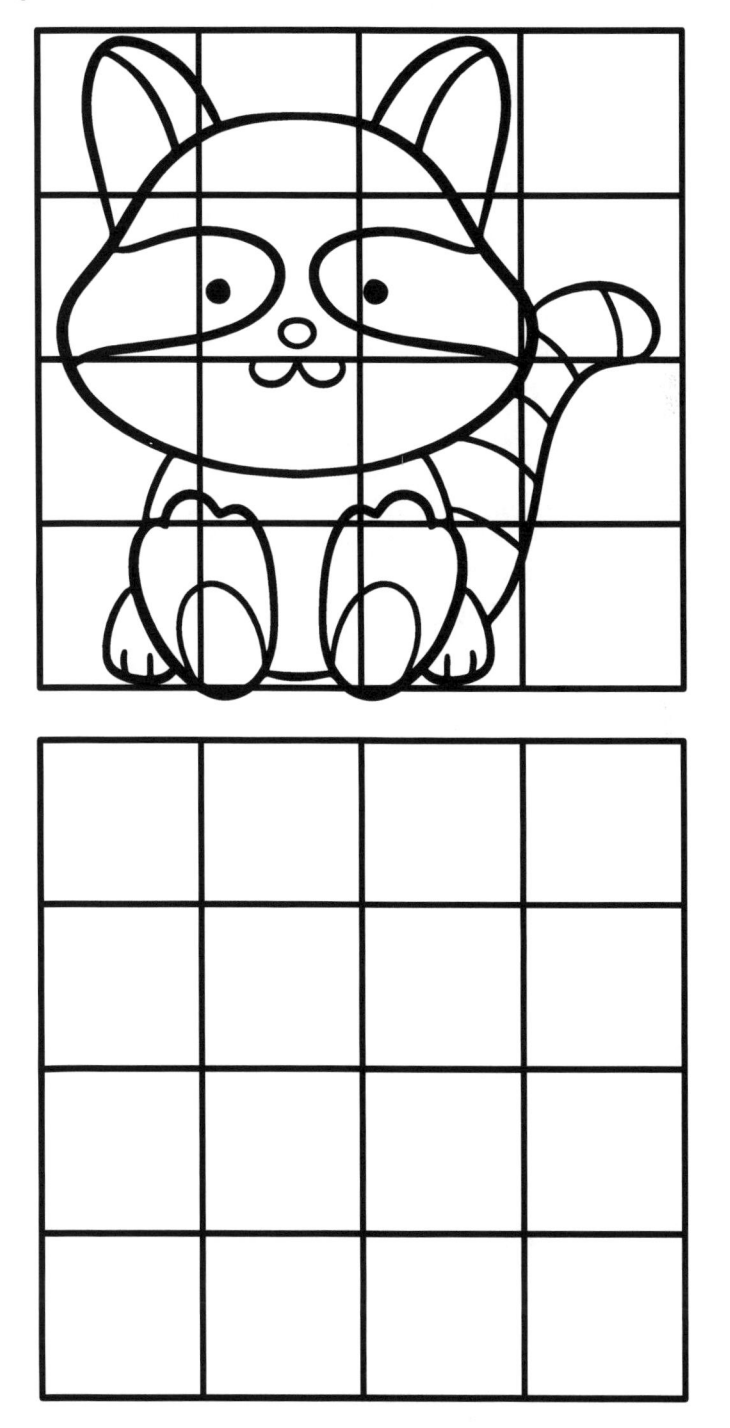

Storytelling

Write an adventure story about a baby deer (fawn), a baby squirrel, and a baby fox.

Tic-Tac-Toe

COYOTE MAZE

Draw a Fawn

Draw the fawn by drawing what you see in each box.

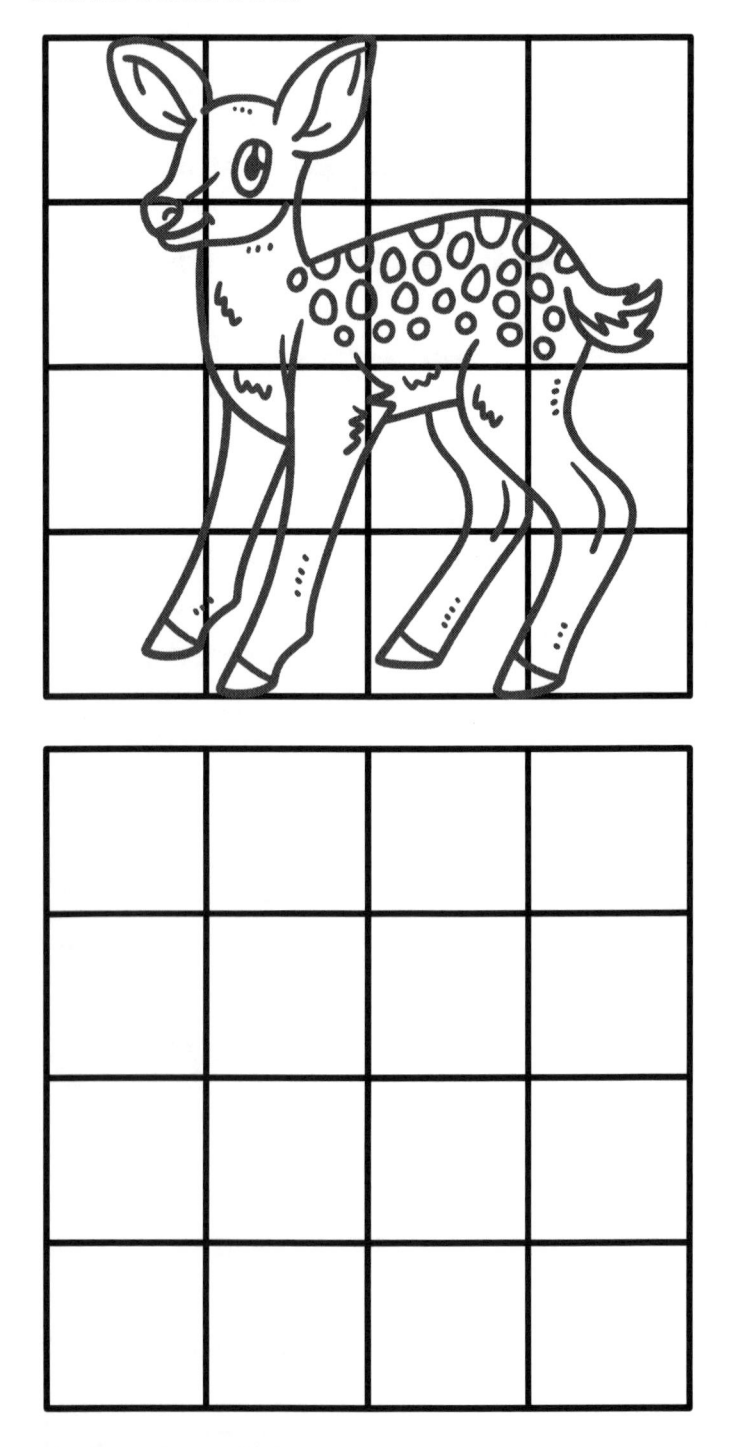

Let's go camping!

Color the things you would take on your camping trip

Word Search

Yosemite's first inhabitants were the indigenous people, the Miwok, Piute, and Ahwahneechee. Find their names and their words for places.

B	T	U	A	M	I	W	O	K	S	A	M	N
I	U	Z	E	R	Y	O	S	E	M	H	T	I
R	H	M	I	K	J	L	A	B	S	W	R	N
D	S	M	A	G	P	I	U	T	E	A	N	D
U	C	A	L	C	L	E	A	E	A	H	I	I
R	Z	T	D	E	H	O	U	N	T	N	C	G
P	P	I	N	E	T	A	E	A	E	E	O	E
S	O	B	A	S	K	E	T	Y	R	E	U	N
D	H	A	L	F	D	O	M	A	F	C	S	O
E	W	A	W	O	N	A	E	E	A	H	I	U
E	U	Z	A	M	A	T	I	K	L	E	Z	S
R	R	A	C	T	U	N	N	E	L	E	T	A

- Wawona
- Uzamati
- Miwok
- Tenaya
- Piute
- Basket
- Umacha
- Indigenous
- Ahwahneechee

Uzamati means grizzly bear. U' macha is the name for the houses the Miwok's built.

Tic-Tac-Toe

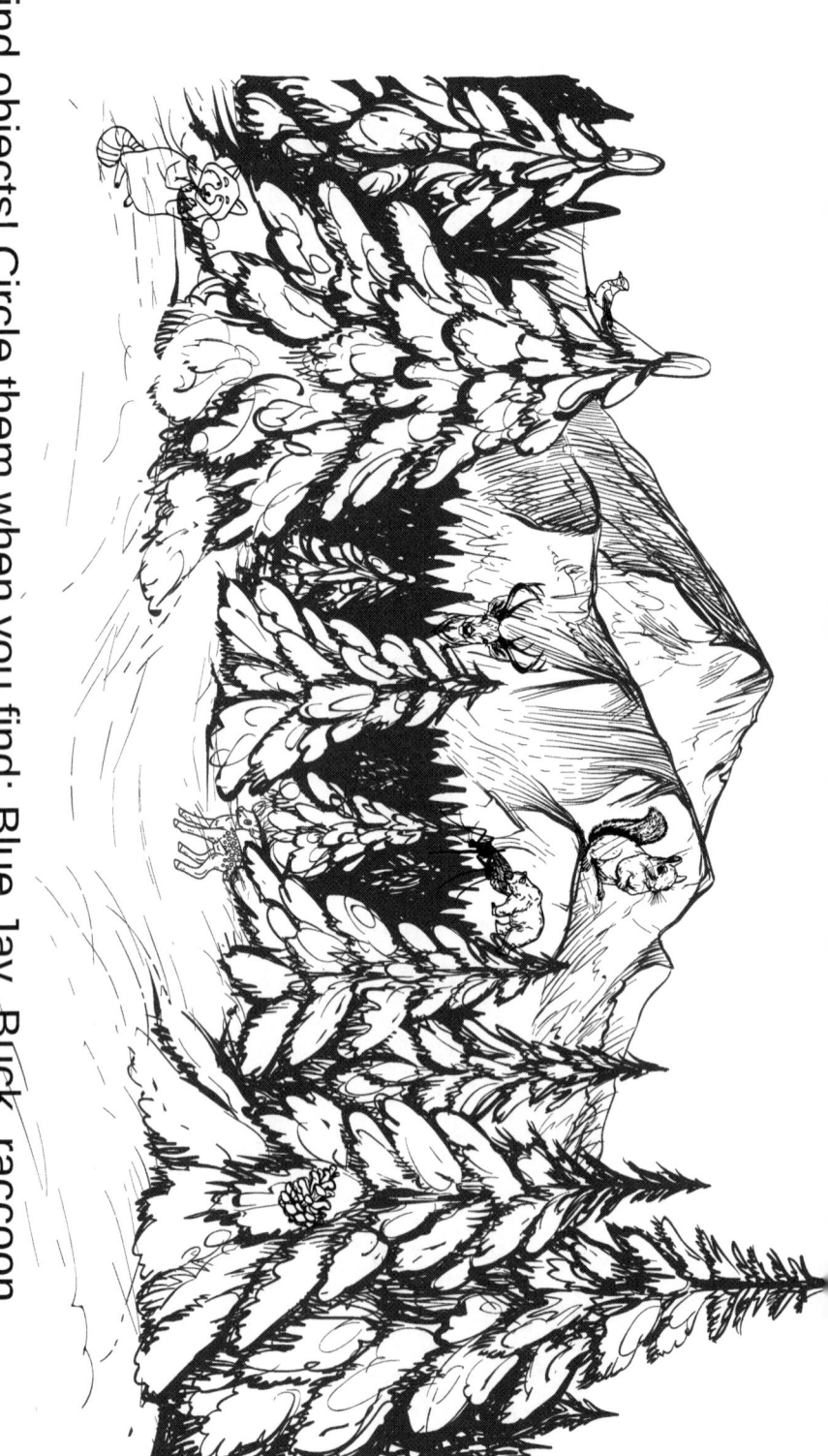

Find objects! Circle them when you find: Blue Jay, Buck, raccoon, Pinecone, mosquito, bear, squirrel, baby deer (fawn).

Journal

write about your trip so you will always remember it!

We rode in a _____ to get to Yosemite. It took us__ days to get here.

Who went with you?

What did you like the most about visiting Yosemite?

Did you camp or stay in a hotel?

What is a funny memory from your trip?

What was the most beautiful thing you saw?

Did you see any animals?

Did you go in the summer, spring, fall, or winter?

What is the best thing you did in Yosemite?

Journal

Add anything else about your trip that you will always remember!

Made in the USA
Las Vegas, NV
16 March 2024